Mutual Funds Investment

Guide To Mutual Funds Investment For Beginners

By : Priyank Gala

Published by:

Priyank Gala

Copyright 2015 –: Priyank Gala

ISBN-13: 978-1517565725
ISBN-10: 1517565723

Table of Contents

Chapter1: Defining mutual funds:

Mutual funds are a type of funds, which comes with various multiple benefits. As we all know there are variety of fund schemes in the market, but mutual funds are amongst the best possible way for even an amateur to invest into. Example: A sum amount of Rs.1, 000/- has to be invested in equity shares by Amit and on looking at the share prices of some of the top-level companies, he comes across a statistic report which shows that probably a BRICK LTD., CONSTRUCTION LTD., HARDWARE LTD., MARBLE LIMITED & a SECURITY LTD COMPANY'S have a share market of 1000, 2000, 400, 300 and 100 respectively. With his budget of just 1,000 he can probably just invest in 2 companies like getting a few shares of the Hardware limited and a few of the Security limited, he is just not allowed to invest in the other companies after choosing one or two companies. He got into a problem when he understood that he could invest in just two companies whereas the best way he read somewhere was diverse investment.

At some occasion on meeting his colleagues during a practice match maybe, he understood that they are also in the same situation with Sandeep having an outlay of 1000, Raj's outlay as 800, whereas Sunny and Farhan just have 500 as their respective outlays, which on summing up is just Rs.3, 800/-.

On knowing that diversification is the key to success in mutual funds, they get in touch with a fund manager Warren, who happens to be their friend. Warren then takes up the total sum and purchases a fund each of the above-mentioned five companies and divides the sum of 3,800/- into 380 units of Rs.10/- each.

With this method, the Net Assess Value (NAV) of each person is determined in which the investment amount is proportionate to the number of units by each individual. Therefore, in the end, according to the sum amount each individual had above, Sandeep and Amit gets 100units which is determined with their sum of Rs.1000 is divided by rs.10/-, whereas Raj gets 80 units on dividing his sum amount of rs.800 by rs.10/-, similarly, Sunny and Farhan get 50 units each on dividing their rs.500/0 by rs.10/-. The investments are made accordingly and on viewing their performance after a month maybe in a business daily, they find that the total return fund value of what they invested id Rs.3, 920/- as the company share prices are now as Construction limited at 2050, Brick limited at 990, hardware limited at 450, Marble limited at 280 and Security limited at 180 respectively, whereas the total number of units are still 380.

Therefore with the new rates of the companies, the new NAV for each individual becomes Rs.10.32/- on diving the total return fund with 380 units.

Thus, each unit has made a profit of Rs.0.32 Paisa in a month. Now, comes the fees of the fund manager i.e., Warren which as we can say is 1.5 percent and on deducting this from the gained amount, the net gain amount comes out to be Rs.0.3152. Now in the end the units held by each person is multiplied by the gain value thus giving Amit, Sandeep, Raj, Sunny and Farhan the amount of Rs.1,031.52, Rs.1,031.52, Rs.825.216, Rs.515.76 and Rs. 515.76 respectively when multiplied by the respective units they had.

Now, if either of them have plans if selling their units, the person would earn profits on each unit as the profit value of Rs.0.3152. whereas the NAV remains unchanged on the selling and exit of any person from this due to the number of units falling proportional.

This looks like a positive scene now, as the NAVs would have had to bear losses if the fund value had fallen below the initial investment i.e. rs.10/-.

Basically, this is an example or illustration of how a mutual fund has its ways of diversifying funds and giving benefits. This was just a scenario of five investors, but there are many more in thousands probably which make up to what is known as a mutual fund house.

One should know that a mutual fund invests in a variety of categories whether equity shares, government or corporate debts, gold or any other available assets. Thus, a mutual fund is a process or a path, which let's individuals invest into a diverse area and also the other classes of assets.

Chapter 2: Pros and Cons:

The Pros:

Professional Money Management:

A fund manager is supposed to manage finances and is trained accordingly, just like a teacher, doctor, architect or an engineer is trained for their fields.

The goals of funds needs to be reflected which is handled with a systematic approach of a consistent investment strategy taken care by fund managers, along with this in order to make investment decisions, economic trends and market monitoring needs to be taken care of by these managers. There is no doubt mutual funds are the escape when you wish to invest in the equity market and are scared due to lack of knowledge.

Diversification:

Depending upon the investment needs, mutual funds come as a rescuer due to the diverse options it has to offer and undoubtedly diversification is the best way out. As an illustration, on a general term a person like Amit can probably invest in just 2 companies or areas at a go, whereas mutual funds investment gives the ability to invest in various other aspects also, thus letting Amit invest in 5 companies depending on the funds invested in. People are generally scared of the losses and thus do not invest on diverse platforms, although, as an example, a Marble factory happens to go into a loss giving the investor loss of funds, but due to the diverse investments, the losses can be compensated with the profit ratio of the other companies the investment has been made into.

Liquidity:

Within a short span of time, on a normal period of three to five days, the investor can redeem the current market value of the mutual funds sold on any business day.

Affordability:

Most funds have expensive initial investments, whereas mutual funds have preferably low initial investment rates, as low as some schemes at probably Rs.500/-.

Convenience:

Monitoring the performance of your mutual funds is easy and the investor is made aware of all the performance notifications, which can also be viewed by them on the business pages and financial websites, whereas other private sector funds just provide the convenience of things and auto renewal or withdrawal and purchase plans plus have automatic reinvestment without the consent of the investor over a particular fund.

Flexibility and Variety:

There are various options to choose funds from, like the combines stocks and bonds, balanced funds or just choose from the conservative sectorial funds, blue-chip stock funds, the modest growth claiming funds or the ones, which have high risk in terms of returns, there are such scopes of flexibility and variety in it.

Tax Benefits on Investment in Mutual Funds:

Tax benefits are also taken care of and offered to the investor like the equity linked savings by certain mutual fund schemes.

Cons:

Along with the benefits of mutual funds, come a few disadvantages also, where the opinions of the mutual fund experts and investors vary. Some point's of the disadvantages are as listed:

Investment Style:

There are active and inactive forms of investment. Active form of investment is when the investor chooses the stocks and the time to buy and sell a particular stock, whereas by letting someone else do it is considered as inactive style of investment. Undoubtedly active style of investment is interesting and has loads of challenges in it, which requires, patience and virtue, along with some timely dedication and knowledge.

Regulation:

Mutual funds come with regulations and restrictions, as an example is that one cannot invest a huge amount of sum in a particular company and has to invest only till the maximum amount permitted, even if the company has a huge sum that can be used to invest in. direct investing route is preferred by the purist equity investors looking to earn by investing in smaller companies.

Fees:

A general fee of approximately 2.5% of the corpus is charged annually in mutual funds, although this fee includes all the administrative and management charges. The post expense unit value is mirrored through the NAV and the fee is deducted directly from the corpus. Through active or direct investment in equities, the fund management fee is waved off since the management is done by you, although the brokerage, demat account and other administrative charges would need to be paid on each transaction made.

Are Mutual funds in India safe and secure?

The history of mutual funds in India is vast and needs to be understood in order to understand how mutual funds work and whether they are safe and secure. To understand it better, division of mutual funds history has been done into 4parts:

- **UTI Phase(1963-1987):**
  UTI is a short form of Unit Trust of India, which happens to be the first mutual fund in India. The scheme has an era spanning from the year 1963-1987, whereas the first scheme was in 1964 known as the unit scheme 1964. Over the tenure or time, an asset of Rs.6.700 Crore was under the management by 1988.

- **The entry of public sector banks and insurance companies phase:**
  This phase is with the time span ranging from 1987-1993. This era got the non-UTI public sector UTI public sector banks and insurance companies to work banks and insurance companies to work and banks namely, State Bank of India (SBI), Canara Bank and Punjab National Bank (PNB) started with mutual funds. Even the LIC and GIC, namely Life Insurance Company and General Insurance Company of India respectively started with the benefits of mutual funds. A growth of eighty fold was seen during the UTI monopoly period with a sum of Rs. 47, 004 Crore at the end of 1993.

- **Entry of private sector and foreign mutual funds phase:**
  This phase was from 1993-2003. The entry of foreign mutual funds and the private sector funds was made in this era. The first mutual funds Regulation was launched in the first year of this era i.e. 1993 by the Indian Government. The SEBI (Mutual Fund) came in 1996 and even now the industry functions on this.

- **UTI Act Repealed:**
  An assured return scheme US 64 was used as a flagship scheme till 2002, in which declaration of NAVs were not on a daily basis. With time, the

dividends were paid through the income and reserves rather than the underlying securities, since the NAV was set artificially. Although this became difficult to pay the dividends by 2002, thus to stop the UTI from further issues in February 2003, the UTI Act was divided into two parts and was repealed.

First:

This represented the UTI with assets managed under Rs.29.835 crores by the end of 2003 January. In broader terms, the US 64 scheme was under the specific undertaking in this scheme and assured returns and other schemes were included. This was excluded from the Mutual Funds Regulations and was functioning under an administrator, which applied the Government of India rules to it. An interest rate of 6.76 percent tax-free was carried under this scheme with a bond of 5 years, where the investors were not permitted to redeem their points.

Second:

This UTI mutual fund works under the Mutual funds Regulations and is SEBI registered, as well as has SBI, PNB, BOB and LIC as sponsors. The current state of growth in the mutual funds industry took place with this move along with the private sector funds being merged with them.

GROWTH IN ASSETS UNDER MANAGEMENT

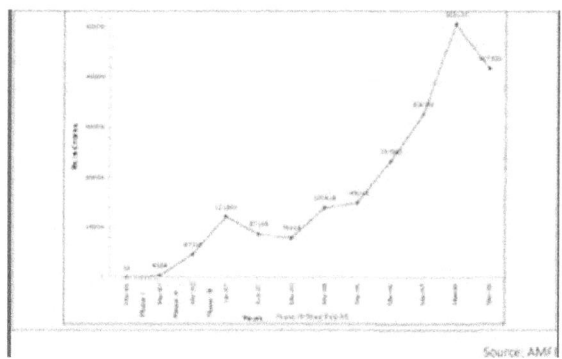

Mutual Funds Regulatory Framework:

The securities market on India is the regulator of the functioning of mutual funds and work under the Securities and Exchange Board of India (SEBI) which have framed strict guidelines and regulatory framework for the functioning of mutual funds. The year 1996 played a role in laying the rules and guidelines by SEBI over the period of time along with the provisions which were related to mutual funds operating system. The mutual funds need to comply with the regulatory provisions of SEBI and submit quarterly report over it every fortnight as an eye through timely reports is always kept by SEBI on mutual funds. The mutual funds every year are inspected under the supervision of SEBI and the needed changes or rectifications are informed on completion. Up gradation of professional standards is taken care by the Association of Mutual Funds of India (AMFI), which also helps in promoting the best possible industry practices since it is an umbrella organization in the category of mutual funds.

Mutual Funds Structure:

There are fours factors that determine mutual funds, which are as follows:

1. Sponsors:

A sponsor is someone who creates a mutual fund. Under the strict guidelines and rules of SEBI, a sponsor appoints a few people for handling the mutual fund, i.e. trustee, custodian, and an asset management company (AMC), although the SEBI standards have to be maintained while creating a mutual fund and maintain problem free funding's, be it in any form like maybe a company, financial or any other institution or a scheduled bank. The AMC takes over the things and the sponsor is left at the position of being a stakeholder and a beneficiary.

2. Fund Manager/ Asset Management Company (AMC):

Management of the mutual fund money is the role of a fund manager. Whether accounting information, NAV calculation, Units pricing information, providing listing schemes or secondary market unit transactions, taking decisions regarding investments or compensating the dividends amongst the investors, all these roles are played by AMC. Quarterly reports are submitted and due diligence on investments are exercised by the AMC. The fund manager is bound by the terms that no other business can be undertaken except that of the managed asset, nor can any other fund be acted upon. The fee on a collection below Rs.100 Crore should not be more than 1.25% maximum and when it is above rs.100 Crore, the fee should be ax 1%.

3. Trustees:

The property of mutual fund unit holders for their benefits is held by the trustees. Although at times the sponsor and the trustee play the same role while handling the market schemes are concerned in order to have approvals, which are secure. The fund's assets need to be protected and are dutifully checked by the investments by AMC which are within the defined limits. The trustees ensure the due returns for the unit holders. The consent of unit holders is needed before the trustees also review taking any major decisions regarding the funds, along with the due diligence handled by the AMC. SEBI receives reports half yearly whereas an annual report is submitted to the investors. A 0.05 percent of weekly average NAV is paid to the trustees annually.

4. Custodian:

The assets and securities are monitored and secured by a Custodian. The trustee and sponsor act as custodians in public sector mutual funds. Collecting income, receiving and delivering securities, unit safekeeping, settling between schemes and distributing dividends are the key roles of a Custodian. A charge of 0.15-0.2 percent of net value of holing is charged by the custodian and more than a single fund can be given service to by them.

Reason behind a complicated mutual fund structure:

The reasoning behind such a complex structure can be found in the recent history of mutual funds. Merrill Lynch had faced the trouble of bankruptcy during the global financial crisis era, which raised questions and concerns over the Investment in DSP Merrill Lynch by Indian investors, but the structure of Indian mutual funds was strong enough to protect the people who had invested in this. Custodian or caretaker of the investment is the trust as we already know, which needs a trust deeds stating "in accordance to the respective schemes,
beneficial interest would be given to the trust holders according to the holding of the individuals as and when the schemes comply', in order to form it.
Trust property proportional to the investment is given as a right to the unit holders. Therefore, even if Merrill Lynch had wrapped up and tried to sell the shares, it would not have been made possible, thus the money would have belonged and returned to the unit holders.
The AMC was provided advisory services by Merrill Lynch by getting into a partnership with the Indian based DSP. Here the AMC acted as a manager for funds giving the right advice on purchase and selling of funds. Thus due to the mutual funds structure no financial loss to DSP Merrill Lynch is caused by the sale of Merrill Lynch AMC to BlackRock.

Chapter 3: Understanding why mutual funds are recommended:

Mutual funds and professional money managers are nearly the same and the fact that these are regulated is a huge thing in favor of mutual funds thus offering the investors the option and way to maintain and evaluate their track record and analyze things. Investment professionals can work easily with funds, whereas mutual funds does not require professionalism in choosing the schemes as it can be learned over a period of time with safe returns.

Investing is becoming more complex:

Things are not as simple as they were sometime back, as people simply understood the market strategy going up and down with the season like monsoon got the market to gain heights whereas Diwali got the market to fall. The Indian stock market started having an impact when the integration of India started with the world with certain factors like the Brazilian currency collapse, or the default on its debt by Russian government, or the short term US interest rates increased and made a huge impact.

Mutual funds provide risk diversification:

The primary portfolio structuring has the tenet of diversification of a portfolio, which is very important when the assumed risk by the portfolio holder is concerned and needs to be at a reduced level. It is better to leave the theories of portfolio structuring in the hands of a professional, as most of the people are not well equipped with the knowledge of applying this theory. Mutual funds are helpful in this regard and let us give the burden to someone else.

Chapter 4: Types of Mutual Funds

Underlying investments are the basic criteria for categorizing Mutual Funds. Closed-ended or open-ended schemes are handles under all mutual funds, thus mutual funds can be classified broadly as:

1. Close-ended Fund (CEF)
2. Open-ended fund
3. Money Market/ Cash/ Liquid Funds:
4. Income Funds
5. Fixed Maturity Plans (FMP)
6. Hybrid/ Balanced Fund
7. Monthly Income Plans (MIPs)
8. Equity Funds
9. Dividend Yield Funds
10. Equity Tax Saver Funds/ Equity Linked Savings Scheme (ELSS)
11. Sector Funds
12. Exchange Traded Funds
13. Gold Funds

1. Closed-ended fund (CEF):

Closed-ended funds also known as CEF as the name suggests are investments, which are frozen or locked during the launch of the fund enrolled for, and a time period is specified according to the offer document. Only during the 'New Fund Offer " NFO period lets investors buy units directly from a fund. After this time period, Transactions can be done through stock market only, whether buying of units or selling them like the usual stock exchange scripts listed. The CEF fund managers have better returns to be provided than the open-ended fund managers, as the pressure of any redemptions or transactions on an ongoing process is not on the CEF managers due to the policies of CEF, while the investor does compromise on liquidity.

2. Open-ended fund:

Under this fund, an investor is open to invest and demand money any time during the scheme. In this, the transaction of money is not as per some rules and regulations of fixed time period, the AMC will accept and return money as and when the investor is willing for it.

Funds are mainly categorized into:
- Debt Funds

- Equity Funds
- Balanced Funds
- Gold Funds

Another category the realtors are talking about is Realty Mutual Funds, which are yet to be implemented in India.

- ***Debt Mutual Funds:***

    Underlying Debt instruments like government securities and bonds are invested into under the debt mutual funds. Portfolio risks can be diversified though Debt Mutual Funds. The investment time horizon and individual risk profile determines the amount that can be invested by an individual in Debt Mutual Funds. It is recommended strongly by financial planners that this is not a tool which should be used for long term wealth creation, rather using it as a risk diversifying tool and value store is better while using the debt instruments. Investment periods of less than 3 years are best suited for debt mutual funds.

    > ***Tips of selecting Mutual Funds:***
    >   - High expense ratios tend to create yield sacrifice, thus expenses are critically important.
    >   - It is not necessary that a small or new debt fund will be risky.
    >   - Yield To Maturity (YTM) has less important than Total return.
    >   - Credit Quality, i.e. the funds is safer when the holding rates are better than others.
    >   - Average Maturity indicates that higher interest rate risk and duration achieves higher average maturity. It should be noted that higher risk is involved in funds, which have higher average maturity than the ones with lower average maturity.

    The relationship between the market price of security and interest rates need to be understood in all categories of debt funds. It is to be noted that the interest rate trend is inversely proportional to the debt instrument price like a bond or a government security, etc. in the country. The security prices in the market will fall when the interest rates are increasing in the market, because demand for existing securities and new issues involving higher interest rates fall when the upward trend in the interest rates are seen. Thus, people buy new issues and existing securities are sold in the secondary market.

On the other hand, the prices take a leap towards increase when the interest rates are on a downward trend, reason being the fact that the demand for existing securities will gain popularity while new issues would carry lower interest rates.

Types of Debt Mutual Funds:

1. *Floating Rate Fund (FRF):*

A fixed rate and fixed tenure is invested upon in securities by the mutual funds house.

Example: A government paper has a rate of return of 3% and a maturity period of 3 years in which a fund may invest, it needs to be noticed that the NAV or the market price is not fixed here, rather the underlying securities coupon rates are fixed. Thus, the value or price of the government paper would fall if the interest rates increase, thus making the debt funds fixed rate take a downfall.

Now, if we consider a floating fund, investment is made in the floating rate instruments and not the underlying fixed rate instruments. Thus, the MIBOR says, that a security, which offers 1% return above the benchmark, can be invested in by the fund. Which in turn, gives the benefit of the interest rates and coupon rates both taking an upward trend while the yield remained untouched.

Best suited for:

This is a wonderful way to use the rising interest rates as it gives good scope of diversifying your portfolio and FRF's perform really well in this situation and secure the short-term returns irrespective of the fluctuations of the interest rates.

Avoid if:

For long-term portfolios, an investor needs to look at other options, as FRFs are best suited for short-term money schemes. Moreover, underperformance may be seen by an FRF while the interest rates are falling.

2. *Gilt Fund*

Sovereign bonds take all the attention and investment from Gilt Bonds. Gilt Funds are basically instrument that bear interest rates and are issued by the government for their borrowing programme.

Best suited for:

Undoubtedly zero risk and high liquidity is carried by government securities, therefore are best suited for the ones who are looking for some security while investing.

Avoid if:
Short-term investments in Gilt Funds are volatile; as sharp and high fluctuations are seen in government securities since interest rate movement have high sensitivity in regards of government securities.

3. **Money Market/ Cash/ Liquid Funds:**
These funds are high on liquidity they offer, due to the investment in short term papers, which are categorized under short-term debt funds. Low expense ratio and higher profile credit quality, needs to be ensured before investing in these funds.

Best suited for:
It comes as the best option when protecting the principal is viewed while investing money for short-term schemes. It is better to invest in this rather than keeping cash lying in a savings bank account, which is not giving any benefit.
Avoid if:

This should not be invested in if the time horizon is more than 3-6 months as these are short-term instruments strictly.

4. **Income Funds:**
Slightly longer tenure bonds are invested into by these funds as and when compared to the money market funds. Growth of capital is not what is looked upon in this, rather current income is primarily looked upon.
Best suited for:

Investing money for approx. an year, this proves to be the safest way. The best time to invest is while the downward trend is seen in the interest rates, although the benefits of this depend on the interest rates condition of the country time to time.

Avoid if:
The return or yield for income funds will be low if the interest rates are high.

5. Fixed Maturity Plans (FMP):

These offer a fixed maturity as they are broadly classified as close-ended income schemes, starting from a period of 15 days and ranging to 2 years or more.

Example: The money is paid back to the investor at the end of a maturity period in an FD, in FMPs basically when the time period ends. Fixed income schemes are invested in by FMP, which are bonds, money market instruments, government securities, etc. just like any other income scheme. The tenure of the scheme decides the tenure of these instruments. Regular income funds are different from FMPs, in regards that maturity of the scheme is taken into consideration in accordance with the securities, which are invested in, so that either before or on the scheme maturity date, the different instruments mature. The investments are rotated depending on the higher yield of instruments by the fund manager, which creates interest rate risk of the fund and is done by the fund manager in an income fund.

It should be remembered that these returns are not guaranteed even though the FMPs mitigate risks at interest rates. The beginning of a term makes the fund manager lock the market prevailing yield, which is done in accordance with the scheme tenure, i.e. the indicative return rate, likely to be received by the fund manager but not guaranteed.

Best suited for:

FMPs give a good way when diversifying the portfolio is concerned, just like all the debt products. Undoubtedly FMPs prove to be the best when working out on tax efficiency when compared to bank deposits, when you fall in the category of 20-30% of higher tax slabs.

Avoid if:

The returned tend to be on a lower side as and when compared to the equity funds, as these are low risk investments. Long-term wealth benefits are not the suitable option for this.

6. Hybrid/ Balanced Fund:

A mix of debt and equity products is invested in through these funds. A strategic allocation is created of both equities and debt equities. The main source behind this is providing growth through equity portfolio and stability through debt portfolio. People who are looking to experience equities and have a decent exposure to them, plus may not want to have an exposure of 100% to the equities are the perfect option for this scheme.

Automatic rebalancing advantage by the fund manager can be enjoyed along with having the control over the exposure level to the asset classes in both the products. This further has tax efficiency for the investors.

This fund is divided into two categories:

Equity Oriented Balanced Fund

Debt Oriented Balanced Fund

At least 65% must be in equities while the remaining in debt where equity oriented balanced fund is concerned. The remaining funds in the debt are categorized under the debt oriented balanced fund. For tax purposes it matters as to what percentage is toward equity orientation, whereas from the investment perspective, it does not make a difference whether it is 50% or 65%. Long term capital gains tax are exempted due to the tax benefits equity oriented balanced funds receive due to the fact that they are treated as equity funds.

Best suited for:

These funds are best when a boost to the portfolio needs to be given without being too sure of equity investments. Stock market participation is possible through these irrespective of the fact that debt portion stability is seen in these funds. Balanced funds can be thought over and invested into when a time span of 4- 7years is available.

Avoid if:

Long-term investments are better done with diversified equity funds, and balanced funds should be avoided if the time span is more than 5-7 years.

7. **Monthly Income Plans (MIPs):**

Providing capital growth and regular income generation are the two aspects of the dual prospective that are offered by MIPs. Debt, equity, money market and equity-oriented are the instruments in which the amount mobilized is generally invested in order to achieve this dual perspective.

Basically, the dual opportunity provided by MIPs are diversified on the basis of enhancing the overall return chances through equity and achieving a steady return through debt portfolio is seen through these ultraconservative balanced funds.

MIPs have different variants, as an example 25-30% exposure to equity is also seen in some MIPs. The exposure level to equities makes MIPs risky, although higher potential returns over a longer time period might be seen in these aggressive MIPs. MIPs who have capped a 1-15% equity exposure would do well when invested in by conservative investor.

Providing attractive returns which are better than the fixed deposits and debt funds is seen by this asset mix over a period of time, whereas short-term returns may see return fluctuations due to factors related to the market scenario.

Best suited for:

This is an option suitable for investing money, which gains regular income, although it should be remembered that monthly dividends may vary according to the market condition and are not given.

Avoid if:

This option is not suitable for wealth creation as an objective and may disappoint you if the dividends are not good at returns as a source of livelihood.

8. **Equity Funds:**

   Stock market investments are done in equity funds.

   Undoubtedly there are numerous types of mutual funds and they need a merit to be well acquainted with, thus understanding the features of equity investing is important before learning the different types of mutual funds. With time, equity investment can show huge and tremendous portfolio growth.

No.	Year	Sensex	1-year (%)	3-year (%)	5-year (%)	7-year (%)	10-year (%)	15-year (%)	20-year (%)
0	31-Mar-79	100							
1	31-Mar-80	129	28.57						
2	31-Mar-81	173	34.9						
3	31-Mar-82	218	25.52	29.58					
4	31-Mar-83	212	-2.85	18.05					
5	31-Mar-84	245	15.99	12.34	19.64				
6	31-Mar-85	354	44.24	17.56	22.43				
7	31-Mar-86	574	62.24	39.45	27.03	28.33			
8	31-Mar-87	510	-11.1	27.66	18.57	21.76			
9	31-Mar-88	398	-21.94	4.02	13.48	12.6			
10	31-Mar-89	714	79.13	7.51	23.79	18.47	21.7		
11	31-Mar-90	781	9.45	15.22	17.15	20.5	19.76		
12	31-Mar-91	1168	49.54	43.12	15.25	24.36	21		
13	31-Mar-92	4285	266.88	81.66	52.97	82.76	34.68		
14	31-Mar-93	2281	-46.78	42.98	41.73	31.76	26.82		
15	31-Mar-94	3779	66.73	47.85	39.54	33.08	31.43	27.37	
16	31-Mar-95	3261	-13.71	-4.7	33.07	35.02	24.85	24.04	
17	31-Mar-96	3367	3.24	13.85	23.55	24.79	19.33	21.84	
18	31-Mar-97	3361	-0.17	-3.83	-4.74	23.16	20.72	20	
19	31-Mar-98	3893	15.82	6.08	11.28	18.75	25.59	21.41	
20	31-Mar-99	3740	-3.92	3.57	-0.21	-1.92	18.01	19.9	19.85
21	31-Mar-00	5001	33.73	14.15	8.92	11.86	20.39	19.3	20.09
22	31-Mar-01	3604	-27.93	-2.53	1.37	-0.67	11.92	19.02	16.38
23	31-Mar-02	3469	-3.76	-2.48	0.64	0.89	-2.09	15.63	14.85
24	31-Mar-03	3049	-12.11	-15.21	-4.77	-1.41	2.95	14.53	14.27
25	31-Mar-04	5528	81.31	15.32	8.13	7.37	3.88	14.62	16.85
26	31-Mar-05	6492	17.44	23.23	5.36	7.58	7.13	15.16	15.66
27	31-Mar-06	11279	73.74	54.66	25.63	17.08	12.85	16.32	16.05
28	31-Mar-07	13072	15.90	33.23	30.38	14.71	14.58	7.72	17.6
29	31-Mar-08	15644	19.68	34.07	38.60	23.83	14.92	13.7	20.14
30	31-Mar-09	9700	-37.99	-4.90	11.90	15.82	10.00	8.45	13.94
31	31-Mar-10	17528	80.70	10.27	21.97	28.38	13.36	11.86	16.83
32	31-Mar-11	19445	10.9	7.52	11.5	19.7	18.36	12.4	13.1
	Probability of loss		11/32	6/30	3/28	3/26	1/23	0/18	0/13
	Average return		27.64	18.84	18.37	19.56	17.05	16.29	16.74

Certain rights and ownership are given when you buy the shares of a company. Adding to it, capital appreciation benefit is achieved when over a time period, the company achieves growth and notices an increase in its share price.

Emerging as strong and getting a tide over interest rate and inflation change can be seen by fundamentally strong companies.

Returns approximately of 15% or more per annum can be witnessed when long-term outlook for equity investments is considered, although, here long-term means a minimum of 10years or more.

This is true although unbelievable, and can be rechecked and reassured by giving a look over different time periods on the returns given by the Sensex-Benchmark index.

Depending upon the period of time invested in equities, the chances of making a loss can be seen. As an illustration, during the period of 1979-2011, if Sensex investments were made, then facing loss in 11 out of the 32 years was sure. But, loss probability would have been near to zero if the time period was over 10years or more, plus giving returns of 16% or more per annum would have been seen.

This return would have on investing in index fund, whereas other diversified equity funds investment would have beat even these returns handsomely.

Tips on equity funds parameters selection:

- Investment objective should be kept in mind while choosing a fund. Depending on the perception of risk, the choice between growth and value should be chosen.
- Funds without any track record should not be picked; rather experienced funds should be invested in.
- Fund managers records should be tracked and experience of fund management should be checked.
- Lower costs are seen in funds, which are large.
- Ratings and rankings, which give risk adjusted returns, should be chosen amongst the plenty of them available.
- It should be ensured that the cash holding percentage is low in equity funds.
- Opportunities get exploited when a higher portfolio turnover is seen where more transactions and costs are involved. Whereas, stable investments and patience is represented by low turnover.

Types of Equity funds:

a) Diversified Equity:

A wide array of stocks is seen in diversified funds. The fund manager in its holdings maintains a high level of diversification, thus the risk in fund is reduced in this manner. In simple terms, the portfolio is designed in such a manner that it is free of domination by any company or any segment dealing in a particular niche.

The freedom of investing in varied market segments and across industries is given to the fund manager, which are the small cap, mid cap and large cap. Although, integral guidelines are set by most of the fund houses for the fund managers, which decide over the maximum exposure they are permitted to in the segment or the industry.

Best suited for:

These funds are the best when long-term creation of wealth is the objective.

Avoid if:
Time period of less than 5-7 years is not the feasible option for this and the funds can be volatile also.

b) **Index Funds:**
This is a passively managed fund and the performance of market index benchmark like S&P CNX Nifty or BSE Sensex is tracked. A portfolio of the same proportion securities is maintained to achieve this intended result as it is in the category of benchmark index. Index fund offer document states very crisply over the fact that tracking would take place for which fund.
Best suited for:
The best part of this is that the exact investment shares of funds is known, besides which a matching index fund portfolio is impossible to be created by an individual investor for his portfolio.
Avoid if:
Above average earning returns are forfeited due to the downside of investing in an index fund, which might be possible through diversified quality fund over a period of long-term.
Actively managed diversified fund and index funds differ from each other in the aspects that trading is done in order to let account redemptions of fresh inflows and outflows take place and not in the terms of making an effort for selling non-performing securities.

9. *Dividend Yield Funds:*
Companies, which have high dividend yield funds, are the places where investment in shares is done by dividend yield funds. The dividend per share, which is divided by the market price of the shares, is what defines dividend yield funds. Stocks having a higher dividend yield than the dividend yield of a particular index, which is Nifty or Sensex, is the area where most of these funds invest in.
Volatility is low for dividend yield stock prices than that of the growth stocks, with the added benefit of earning appreciation being a potential aspect, are also a good thing to mention and keep in mind. When a business has enough cash generation, it means the dividend payout is high.
Best suited for:
Investors who wish to diversify their portfolio within the segment of

equity funds, and wish to receive regular dividends, dividend yield funds are amongst the best options due to the fact that they have a medium risk proposition within the space of equity funds.

Avoid if:

Short-term corrective phases have not always been the right option for dividend yield funds due to their bad history of not always being resilient to these phases.

10. Equity Tax Saver Funds/ Equity Linked Savings Scheme:

In order to save taxes under the Section 80C of the Income-Tax Act, investors look at equity-linked savings scheme or ELSS for their benefits. The fund manager looks to provide long-term appreciation of capital by investing in instruments related to equity or invest directly into equities under ELSS. The perfect way for capital market participation is ELSS while you can save on some taxes too, due to the potential which ELSS consists of for giving returns which are better than the instruments related to tax saving.

The fund manager has enough time to work upon improving the return capacity and building a good portfolio since the lock-in-period of ELSS is 3years. Investing through Systematic Investment Plan (SIP) in an ELSS, the rupee cost averaging can be taken as an advantage by the investor and not need to put in an investment at the end of a financial year, which is of a lump sum amount.

Best suited for:

These funds are ideal when the objective is saving tax and looking for wealth creation, which is for a long-term.

Avoid if:

These funds may turn out to be volatile if the time period of investment is less than 5-7 years, although it is said that the lock-in period is of 3years, but the best result is achieved mostly after 5-7years.

11. Sector Funds:

As the name suggests, these funds aim a particular industry for their investments and are highly focused. If the timing is right, due to the fact that market cycles are what the sector funds ride on, they have the potential of offering returns which are good since the basic aim of this is to give investors the industry cycles advantage.

Best suited for:
Sector funds hold higher risks as and when compared to diversified fund, therefore should hold or constitute a small or limited portfolio portion. Moreover, only investor with an existing portfolio should think of investing in these.

Avoid if:
As mentioned above, that the investment is at a particular industry or sector, thus are not diversified and therefore the downside risk protection which can be seen in diversified fund cannot be availed in Sector funds.

12. Exchange Traded Funds (ETF):

The combined features of, stocks and index funds is what makes a hybrid product called an Exchange Traded Fund (ETF). The prices of these funds are linked to the underlying index while they are listed on the stock exchanges, also letting the market makers for ETFs be the authorized participants.

ETF functions like any other stock where the selling and purchasing is considered and can be processed at market hours at the prices closer to NAV during the day end. The way open-ended schemes function, similarly, investment can be made at real time process as against the end of the day prices. ETF investments need 2 accounts, i.e. demat and the trading account. These funds are managed passively and have the benefits of administrative charges, which are minimal and the distribution cost is also low. Thus, the expense ratios for ETFs are lower as and when compared to other funds.

Best suited for:
Due to the benefits of trading in stocks, although they are mutual funds, they give dual benefits.

13. Gold Funds:

Other that the above mentioned 2 categories of mutual funds, i.e. debts and equity, another asset class category i.e. Gold also exists. There are options of investing in Gold and golf funds, so let us look at investment in Gold before we proceed with Gold funds.

Pros & Cons of Gold:

Pros: A physical asset, which can be seen, felt or touched and has high liquidity due to the fact that it's a precious metal. It has no risk of credit and is worn as a jewelry plus adding an aesthetic value due to it. Gold does not have the risk of bankruptcy or shutting down which can be seen in banks or corporate when badly managed.

Cons: The utility value for gold is not high, and cannot yield intermediate cash flow like the equity shares or the real estate's dividend generation. Thus, like equity shares can be put a value upon, it is not a case in gold.

Does Gold give good returns?

We need to look at the history of 31years for gold prices globally as RBI website takes care and sets the gold prices. USD 208 per troy ounce was the price of gold in London in the years 1978-79, which took a rise to USD 1023 by the years 2009-10, thus the CAGR or the annualized average yield came out to be 5.27% per annum. An assumed CAGR of 6.14% for the year 2010-2011 is noticed, as the official record is unavailable.

Now, if we take a look in India, the average gold price (Mumbai) for 1gms was Rs. 791/- in the year 1978-79, which in turn changed to Rs. 15.756 for 10gms by the year 2009-10, thus working out an annualized yield of 10.13% per annum. Now the average rate assumed for the year 2010-11 has been Rs. 19,000/- with the CAGR at 10.44%.

As we can see the difference of 4.3%, now what might be the reason behind this? The reasoning here is that this amount is calculated on the basis of dollar against rupee appreciation. Thus, we have earned following this, an appreciation of 4.3% in dollar and 6.14% in gold due to the fact that we Indians have always believed that we are investing in gold whereas we are actually investing in dollars.

Another question, which follows this theory, is that fact that what happens if we earn 6.14% from gold and 4.3% for dollar?

As we see the history of 31 years, many global factors influence the dollar and approx. 5% per annum appreciation has been seen by dollar in these many years. It is not known whether the dollar or the gold would recover and have better future prospects. But, an observation should be made that, a peak of USD 513 was seen by gold in 1980-81, due to the fact that dollar lost its faith during the Vietnam War and other factors, thus making people buy gold and believe it as a safer avenue. The dollar recovered after sometime, whereas the gold never lost its value and stayed in USD 350-400 range. Moreover, the dollar being weak, also gave gold high peaks recently.

Thus, 15-20% of the portfolio should be the maximum where gold should be restricted, even though gold holds an important hedge of the portfolio.

Now, this proves that Gold ETF is probably the best way to invest in Gold.

Gold ETF, what is it?

- The returns of physical gold and gold ETF are nearly the same. Basically, a scheme of mutual fund in which paper or dematerialized form holds the investments made in gold, just like in stocks.
- Gold ETF gives investor units for their holdings in it and stock exchange is the platform where they are listed and traded.
- Advantages like safety, tax benefits, liquidity and cheaper than physical gold purchase is seen with gold fund.

Benefits on the cost aspect:

- **Purchasing Gold**: making charges of around 15-20% is levied on buying gold, whereas this can be excused with just paying a entry load of 2.5% during the New Fund Offer (NFO) by purchase of units. Brokerage charge between 0.5%-1% of the transaction value is charged if the units are purchased after the scheme has been listed.

- **Recurring charges**: a charge of 1% is levied as annual expenses every year in ETF whereas storage and insurance costs are seen in order to maintain the jewelry made through gold.
- **Selling gold**: a brokerage of 0.5%-1% is charged during the exit in ETFs, whereas a percentage of 25-50 is deducted while selling gold jewelry.

Tax efficient: Gold ETFs do not attract any wealth tax as we see wealth tax been charged in case of physical gold.

- A dividend distribution tax of 14% has to be paid by the fund house while tax-free dividends are seen in the investor's hands.
- Long-term capital gains of 20% is seen when the units being sold have been held for more than a year, whereas a holding period of 3 years is needed in case of physical gold in order to get LTCG tax.

Best suited for:

Wealth preservation and reducing portfolio risk are the benefits given by Gold. Assets like the equity and debt, have different ways of acting when compared to gold, it is only gold which help during financial crisis and act as a safe haven too. For example, a fall of 54.75% was seen along with a growth of 29.18% in gold, reason being that people invested their sum of money in gold to save and preserve it in 2008, thus 54.75% of loss would have been seen and experienced if all the money was invested in Sensex in this year. Whereas a reduction of 50.55% would have been seen if gold investment of 5% and remaining amount in equities was made, as in this case, the impact would have been reduced by gold. The mitigation of risk would have been better when the allocation towards gold would have been higher. As an instance, if 25% of investment was made in gold instead of 5% in the year 2008 was made; the total loss seen would have been 33.77%. The same thing can be observed and seen in the reverse scenario. Chances of profits reduce, when exposure to gold is high during the booming market of equity. A recommendation by financial planners is made recommending a portfolio exposure of 5-15% in gold.

Avoid if:

When the objective is long-term wealth creation, sole investment in gold is not recommended; rather it should be used as means of hedge portfolio risks.

Chapter 5: Things to Remember Before Investing

Selecting a mutual fund:

Investing in mutual funds has similar requirements of strategic inputs like the other investment options, but the added advantage here of the asset allocation plan has a strategy, which is a natural extension.

The following process is recommended in money control:

- Asset allocation needs should be seen and observed while investing and identifying funds.
- Mutual funds, which are capable of suiting and handling the risk factors and have tolerance towards them, should be handles just like choosing a laptop suiting our budget and needs.
- Fixed income or equity, sector-focused or general equity, high or low risk, turnarounds or blue chips and short-term or long-term liquidity focus are included in the objectives of typical investment.
- *Consistency should be seen and past performance should be evaluated:* it is a useful way of knowing the good and bad about a fund as compared to others, although there is no guarantee of the future in regards of past performance. Identifying the best of the 5 performing funds over various time periods is a good way of achieving this. Now, check the performance consistency and see the ability.
- *Diversify:* opt for 2-3 mutual funds and not just invest in a single fund, depending on what matches the investment objective and spread the investment. On choosing 2 funds, a split of 60:40 is recommended, whereas 50:30:20 split is recommended on choosing 3 funds at a time for investments.
- *Consider costs of fund:* Investment cost needs a lot of consideration and is definitely a significant factor in case of mutual funds investments, fixed income funds being a specialty in this. A signification portion of the returns can be taken away by sales load, annual expenses of 0.6% and management fees of 1% of the fund. This fee is termed as LOAD.

Invest, review and Monitor:

Management and performance should be monitored when mutual fund investment is made and it should be seen whether the expectation are exceeded or lagged upon. Reviewing mutual funds is required on a lesser frequency maybe, just quarterly, unlike the individual stocks and bonds.

Whether the objective of mutual fund is of selling or investing, the funds performance review should be carried out in accordance to it. If either of the below mentioned events take lace, the mutual funds investments might need to be sold:

- *Investment plan is changes*, as an example, conservative plans might be chosen, as you grow old.
- *The strategy of a fund is changed itself.* This is because the objective of the fund has altered and may not fit the objective it was chosen for.
- *Persistence of poor results of a fund.* The poor result is a proof of lack of expertise by an asset management company and should be replaced by investing in similar securities.

Now, after all the discussions and detailing's, it is a known fact that a process is followed while investing in mutual funds and not just making a decision is enough, therefore, let profits come by following these steps.

Chapter 6: Choosing the right fund:

Selecting a mutual fund requires strategy and not just blind investment in the best performing fund. Like every investment fund needs planning and strategies are involved, similarly mutual funds also require strategies. A simple 4step process can help making the right decision:

1. **Objectives of the asset allocation and mutual funds should match each other and the fund should be identified accordingly:** Every investor has objectives while investing in funds, and there is no point investing in a fund, which does not fulfill the objective in place. As mentioned before in Chapter 1, financial goals should be where the investments should be aligned towards, thus equity funds are the best when the goal is for more than 10years.

2. **Past performance should be evaluated for consistency:** It is important to look at how a fund has performed over the past with the promised things in it, even though the future does not depend on the past performance. The best possible way of achieving this is to find out the best matching funds according to the objectives, and shortlist from them, then look at the time horizons over which they have performed, plus have they been consistent performers and what has been the feedback for them.

3. **Diversification is important:** it is best to pick 2 or 3 mutual funds than finalizing on a single fund, so that the risk of dependency of a single fund can be avoided. The funds should be chosen based on the criteria that the investment objective of each asset allocation is matched, thus spreading the investment.

4. **Cost funds should be considered:** An asset management charge of 1-2.5% is charged every year for funds, thus due consideration needs to be given to the investment cost and due consideration is needed.
   The data of the exit loads and expense ratios of schemes is readily available in the prospectus and the lower expense ratio schemes should be looked upon.

Are MF rankings right and worth being trusted?

Various research firms give out rankings and ratings every quarter, so that their importance and specialty can be proved from the others. All statistical tools and esoteric techniques are used to give dissimilar results by these agencies.

If we take two schemes A and B, lets say, the top of one list is scheme A, whereas other list might have scheme B as its favorite. A new investor might not see a difference, although the method of investing varies. Sharpe or the Sorting ratio might be used as a ranking parameter or even the annualized returns might be used for the same. All of these leave the investor confused, despite of having a justification of own.

Now, comes the issue of trusting ratios or what an investor should do, as it is an important fact that these ratings should not be ignored and should be taken into consideration. Some tips on reading through these rankings are:

- Rakings over a 3year period should be considered and the rakings made on monthly, quarterly or half yearly basis should not be trusted, thus, any ranking under 1year basis can be ignored.
- The rankings are important to be considered and it is best to search and shortlist the mutual funds which rank amongst the top 10 positions in the rankings all around.
- It does not matter much if the top ranking fund in a year slips to the 3rd or 4th position, but the consistent ranking amongst the top 5 is an important aspect to take into consideration.
- In the end, performance of the fund should also be considered before investment.

Financial Planning and Mutual Funds:

Every goal has a mutual fund for it, just like we can relate every occasion with a song.

- Liquid or short-term debt funds can be chosen for **Contigencies** due to their nearly negligible lock-in period.
- For Low risk options, which are 1 to 3 years away, income funds should be considered. Floating rate funds should be considered in the rising interest rate scenario, whereas, pure income/ bond funds should be invested in with falling interest rates, for at least a year.
- For slightly high risk options, which are 1 to 3 years away, balanced or hybrid funds should be invested in.
- A combination of debt and equity funds should be invested in for goals over a period of 3-6 years.
- The best option is equity based funds, when long term goals and high risk taking ability is present, as equity has generally outperformed all other classes of assets over longer durations.

- Equity diversified funds are the best option when someone is new to investing in equity.
- Sector specific or thematic funds like it, Pharma, Auto, etc., should be moved to after experience and confidence in large cap companies is gained.

Chapter 7: Methods of Investing in Mutual Funds:

1. **Systematic Investment Plan (SIP):**
   Principle of regular investments is seen in SIP. A small amount is invested every month just like any recurring deposit. Instead of a one time heavy investment, which might be a problem for some people, SIP helps in accumulating amount in short and small installments, made every month or on quarterly basis.

   Example: An investment of Rs. 10,000/- has to be made, but instead of investing the total amount in MF together, 10 periodic investments of Rs. 1000/- each can be made through SIP.

   Compounding to the maximum can be achieved along with availing and realizing the benefits of it, as through SIP, an average man can make investment of Rs. 500 or Rs. 1000/- periodically.

   A habit of saving can be seen through SIP, although these small investments do not look appealing initially, and these small saving can be beneficial over a period of time.

   Example: Investing Rs. 1000/- monthly in SIP, after 10years would give Rs. 6.69 Lakhs at the rate of 9%, and in 30 years, it would be Rs. 17.83 lakhs and Rs. 44.20 Lakhs in 40 years.

   Investment made at the wring timing can make even the rich lose their sleep n face losses, thus making it important to completely understand and work on the concept of power of compounding and rupee cost averaging, so that SIP working can be better understood.

2. **Discipline:**
   Investment pattern required discipline, focus and regular investments as its cardinal rule for better corpus building. It is easier to invest small amounts every month than huge one-time investments, as small portions would not affect the monthly budget much.

3. **Power of Compounding:**
   The gurus or masters of investments, benefits of compounding being one of the main reasons behind it, always recommend early investments.

   Example: Person X and Person Y make investments of Rs. 10,000/- p.a, X at the age of 30 and Y at the age of 35, now at the age of 60, X has a corpus of Rs. 12.23lakh, whereas Y has a corpus of Rs. 7.89lakh, which is at the rate of interest at 8% assumption. Thus, due to the gap of 5years by Y and an investment of 50,000 lesser than X, made Y lose approx. Rs. 4lakh, making it obvious that the returns are higher when the compounding period is longer.

Now, if we look at another prospective of investment, if X invests Rs. 50,000 after 5 years instead of yearly investment of Rs. 10,000/-, gives him a corpus of Rs. 10.43lakh, as he lost on the power of compounding in the early 5 years.

4. **Rupee Cost Averaging:**

Investment in equities make rupee cost averaging true. More units can be bought at lower prices when investing the same amount at regular time intervals is done in a fund, thus reducing the average cost per unit or share over the time. This explains 'Rupee Cost Averaging'. The risk of investments in volatile markets can be seen along with smoothening the up's and downs of the market by the Rupee Cost Averaging, though a sensible approach in long-term investments.

The lows and highs of the market can be captured and taken care of through SIP investment. Due to the fact that all the phases of the market is seen and gone through whether bull or bear, the average cost of investing comes down. Best results are achieved when all the market conditions are passed through in an SIP, whereas, breaking or stopping an SIP through a bear or bull phase of market, would only reduce or carry off the SIP objective.

5. **Convenience:**

Enrollment form along with cheque needs to be submitted to make it easier and convenient for investing. The units would be credited to the investors account, as the cheque would be submitted on the requested date, thus sending the confirmation to the investor about it, also giving the option of Even Electronic Clearing (ECS).

The method of First-In-First-Out (FIFO) will be used when units are sold for capital gains tax, i.e. the units, which are sold first will be the earliest purchased units.

6. **Systematic Withdrawal Plan (SWP):**

Installments are pre-determined for periodic intervals and money can be withdrawn accordingly from a mutual fund, although the benefit here is that, the investor can choose the intervals and quantum of fund withdrawals.

Meeting monthly expenses can be a challenge but SWP might prove to be a beneficial alternative than the dividend option, as the timing for payouts is selected manually and fund declaring is not the option one needs to wait for. Periodic booking of profits can also be achieved through SWP.

There are 2 types of SWPs:

a) *Fixed SWP:*

With the process of systematic withdrawals, fixed SWP lets one receive a fixed amount of money over the time period specified.

Example: For a time period of 1 year, monthly income of Rs. 2,000/- can be received through fixed SWP.

b) *Appreciation SWP:*

The extent of price appreciation is seen, and automatic withdrawal is allowed through Appreciation SWP.

Example: a trigger of Rs. 55 NAV is set for a mutual fund and it reaches around Rs. 60 per unit, the price appreciation of Rs.5 is achieved and paid to the investor automatically.

One must remember that a sale is considered whenever withdrawal from a fund is made, as this method is only for one's convenience.

7. **Systematic Transfer Plan (STP):**

Periodic transfers from one to another fund can be made through STP.

Example: an equity fund gave a profit of Rs. 60,000/- to an investor, and then the investor wishes to use this profit and keep them in safer investment option like maybe a debt fund, STP helps in achieving this. Thus, fund investments over a time period can be rebalanced or phased out through STP schemes.

Again, the types of STP's just like SWP's are:

a) *Fixed STP:*

At periodic time intervals, fund transfer of a fixed income can be made from one to another fund through fixed STP.

b) *Appreciation STP:*

When a limit set by the investor is crossed by the capital appreciation, this gets activated.

Again as mentioned before, any withdrawal or transfer in tax benefits, is considered as sale or new investment, as these are just methods of making investments convenient.

Advantages:

Funds can be phased out over a time period and periodic transfer of funds from one to another can achieve portfolio rebalancing.

As it is said too many choices can confuse the human mind and create a fuss with things, whether it is buying a pair of denims or maybe choosing amongst the pizza toppings. Thus, when thrown a huge variety of options to choose from by the mutual fund agent, the investor can feel confused and helpless.

Dividend Payout, Growth and Reinvestment are the 3 options offered by Mutual Funds, and each has its own advantages and disadvantages.

a) **Dividend Payout:**

The profit share in a fund, which is paid out to the investor is called a dividend.

Example: The face value of each unit is Rs. 10 for a Mutual Fund worth 100 units, a dividend of 50% is declared by the fund house, now a profit of Rs. 5 is achieved on every unit, thus making it Rs. 500 for 100 units of the mutual funds.

Now the reality here is, that the investor might feel happy over achieving good profits, whereas the truth is that the investor receives his own money back in a different way as the amount of the dividend declared would make the unit fall exactly according to it. Thus, a fall to Rs. 10 would be seen in the NAV if the dividend payout is Rs. 5, provided before the dividend is declared, the NAV was Rs. 15/-.

Now, this is how the option of Dividend payout works.

Tax Implication:

Tax-free dividend funds are achieved in balanced or equity funds. Although, where debt funds are considered, there's a little difference. A dividend distribution tax of 12.5% (surcharge and cess excluded) has to be paid by the mutual fund house when a dividend is declared by the debt fund, when the individuals are paid the dividends. The returns bear the distribution tax on dividends, even though tax on dividend does not need to be paid by the unit holder.

Best for:

When the objective is to get cash at intervals, this is the best option. The dividend payout will always be uncertain and there will never be any surety of announcements of dividends by MF.

Avoid if:

This option is best avoided if periodic money is not the objective. As, long-term returns may not be good and might be interfered with on choosing the dividend payout option.

b) Dividend Reinvestment:

The paid dividend is re-invested in the same scheme with this option.
Example: as we used the example above, the reinvestment would be made instead of paying the amount of Rs. 500 as a dividend. Thus, new units will be bought by using this re-investment and additional units would be present in the fund.

Tax implication:

Capital gains are the only tax impact in this option as the investor's hands hold tax-free dividends. When equity funds are considered under this option, a capital gains tax of 15% will have to be paid when units are sold in a time period of less than 1 year, whereas it is tax-free when the units are sold after a year. Each reinvested dividend makes a calculation being made separately for the time periods. Although, a different scenario is seen with debt funds and tax would depend on the tax slab if the time period of selling units are below an year and selling after a year would make the investor pay 20% as long-term capital gains tax.

Tax deduction on reinvested dividends is also seen as a benefit in this option but only in the ELSS scheme. The section 80C makes the reinvestment be considered as an additional investment.

Best for:

This option is best suited for tax benefits as explained before that the section 80C helps in achieving tax benefits, which are additional.

c) Growth:

Dividends are not paid through the option of growth, unlike the reinvestment or payout options. Rather, the NAV reflects the price appreciation, thus if a appreciation of 5% is seen, the growth of Rs. 10 to Rs. 15 will be seen in the NAV.

Tax implication:

Capital gains tax is the important tax, which needs to be considered in growth funds, i.e. when the units are sold, a tax is charged on the profits achieved through it.

In equity funds, short-term capital gains tax of 15% has to be paid when the units are sold before a year, whereas there is no long-term tax when the units are sold after a year. Although, tax of 20% (with indexation) as long-term capital gains is charged, whereas regular tax slab is for short-term capital gains is taken into consideration.

Best for:

This can be considered and is ideal for long-term goals. The counterparts, i.e. payout and reinvestment options are outperformed by growth due to the fact that in the long run NAV moves up.

P.S.: Dividend Distribution Tax (DDT) on the declared dividends has to be paid by the fund house in the case of debt funds. The return would have a bearing of DDT even though the investor does not have to pay tax. Thus, the score of growth is higher than the dividend reinvestment option, where debt funds are concerned, this is because dividends would bear tax (indirectly) and the tax is seen on the capital also when the reinvestment option is chosen.

Chapter 8: Common Mistakes involved in Mutual Fund Investment:

- The stress of research and picking stocks is avoided by mutual fund investments. But a fault here can give bad results and losses.

- Investors make the mistake of investing or buying mutual funds when the prices are high, although everyone waits for discounts to start for shopping, but some investors don't realize it in terms of mutual funds. Funds should not be bought when the NAVs are have gone up, but the market buoyancy makes the investors forget this rule and invest.

- It is difficult to know the right time without experience in the market and the right NAV of a fund is difficult to find.

- Equity funds investments should have a long-term view of 3-5years at least.

- Short time intervals spurt up the prices, thus value of a well-diversified portfolio increases over a time period, despite of ups and downs.

- SIP's can help reduce the risks of the ups and downs seen in the market.

- Investors thinks that NAV is low, means the fund is cheap, i.e. for example, NAV of a fund was cheap at Rs. 10, and investment was made taking this into consideration, it is again a mistake. It is the portfolio which maters, thus in order to achieve the same growth or returns, a well-diversified portfolio is the best.
  Example: An amount of Rs. 10,000/- has to be invested. There are 2 funds, A and B. On investing in fund A which has an NAV of Rs. 10, an allocation of 1000 units is made, which gives Rs.11 for each unit, thus making it Rs. 11,000/- by a growth of 10%, whereas fund B has its NAV as Rs. 50, thus an allocation of 200units is given. Now, each unit would be at Rs. 55 each, thus making it Rs. 11,000/-. Now the value achieved is the same in both, thus making it clear that cheap NAV is not what needs to be considered.

- The type of fund is not understood, as the risk profile is different for each individual. The fund should be understood and picked according to an individual's profile. Variety of focused funds like the mid-cap and sector funds are flooding the market these days, but the investor should think again before investing in the favorites at the current time. Investment in these should be made only when there is knowledge of financial understanding for taking sector calls.

- Paying attention to the returns of just one year is again a mistake as good returns are given by mutual funds over a long time period, especially in equity funds. It is important to look at the history of a fund over a couple of years, as a fund might have performed bad over the other years except the one year being looked upon and vice-versa. Thus, the performance over a 5year period at least should be considered for better consistency knowledge.

- Selling and keeping the wrong mutual funds, as in selling away the funds which would be beneficial, and keeping the funds which might not give good results. It is important to recognize which fund performs well and which is a loser.

- Distributor's Kick Backs should not influence the investor, which on a general level takes place. Just like everyone else, distributors use kickbacks as a bait for the investor in order to earn for themselves and give false hopes, but the investor should understand and see through it to avoid being captivated through it.

- Portfolio churning should be avoided, even though the distributors would suggest selling the active funds to buy new ones as they get a commission whenever a fresh fund is invested in. performance statistics will be used to convince the investor, but one must know that the statistics can be manipulated.

- Trying to earn fast money is also a bad option as making someone rick overnight is impossible for any fund. The mutual fund distributors show the investor some past data or statistics to woo the investor by showing that the amount was doubled within a very short time, but it is all just a gimmick to sell mutual funds. It might have been true in the past, but that does not mean, the future is also supposed to be according to that. Nothing is better than long-term investments.

- Mutual fund NFOs and Equity IPOs are compared and should not be, because the investor's perception of the share worth value decides the issue price of equity share IPO and then the market value listing of the share is made. Although mutual fund NFOs work on a different principle, as the fund might not be at its best or premium when declared. The reason behind this is that whether NFO or any scheme which is already existing, the mutual funds value is marked to the market. He market price at the investment time is the place where investment in equity shares is made, of the amount collected through NFO or other ways.

  Thus, as an example, an investment of Rs. 20 is made in an NFO unit between the closing dates of issue and first NAV declaration, and the growth of 20% is seen in the share investment, the scheme would list at Rs. 24/-. One should not expect premiums, which are higher from the equity share IPOs.

  The mutual fund managers claim product innovations, which are brought out by NFOs, but the availability of these products might be fake. For example, mid-caps investments would be forced by the mid-cap fund through this. NFOs are just old food packaged in a fresh paper in the case of diversified equity funds.

  Example: a multi-cap fund might be announced when a fund house has a portfolio already consisting of a diversified fund. A mix of small-cap, mid-cap and large-cap funds is what makes a multi-cap fund.

  The best way to increase the size of a corpus is through NFOs. The investor perceives NFOs to be cheap and therefore they are easy to be sold off. Plus as an additional factor, good rewards are given to the NFO distributors as more leeway is given for the expenses of NFO distribution thus, making the distributors get higher applications for it.

The Dividend Bait:

Another popular mutual fund is the dividend bait, and thus investment in a particular fund would be suggested by the agent, as the 'inside' information is available with him regarding the declaration of dividends. A return of Rs. 6,000 is likely to be achieved over a months time on investment of Rs, 20,000/-. Now, the hidden part here is that the amount being paid back is none other that dividend, and this dividend is deducted and subtracted through the fund NAV, thus showing a drop to Rs. 14,000 on investment of Rs. 20,000/-.

What's the difference here?

There are loads of people who can advice over what to buy and what not to buy when it comes to funds. Though seeking advice is a good option, but beware of the people who have half or false knowledge about the market and give advice just for the sake of it, as it is important to know what the truth is and what can be beneficial for ourselves, thus one should be well educated before investing.

Tips on avoiding common mistakes and stay focused:

1. ***The time for returns should be decided upon:***
   - Debt Funds should be invested in, if the time period for return is less than 3 years.
   - Balanced fund is the right choice when the time period is not less than 7years.
   - Equity funds are best when the time period is longer than 7years as long time periods give handsome returns through equities of approximately 15-18% yearly.

2. ***Research is important:***
   - A track record, which is proven for funds, should be invested in.
   - Returns of 5years at least should be seen.
   - Quarterly or half yearly reports should not be trusted, rather consistent performance over 5years or more should be considered for investment.

3. ***Small investments make a difference:***
   Don't wait to collect a huge amount for investing, rather start with small portions.

4. ***Choose the systematic investing route:***
   There is nothing better than the systematic investment route, which is known by the mutual fund agents.

5. ***Regular investment:***
   Small investments are easier and convenient than high portions and will allow regular investments.

6. Don't Panic:

It is normal for fluctuations to take place in the market, there is no need to panic due to it. It is important to realize that equity funds are for long terms and give profits, so don't panic and let your agents make you churn on the investments made.

7. Do not blind trust the agent:

Never trust the agent blindly, as its their job to sell MF schemes with fake promises. Even if a guarantee of 50-100% is being promised by the agent, don't let him make a fool of you, and ask him to write it down, sign it and then purchase, if the agent fumbles while doing this, the answer is clear and evident.